S0-BDK-706

ABOUT THIS BOOK

Anne Simpson and her husband Robert co-authored the book *Through the Wilderness of Alzheimer's: A Guide in Two Voices*, published by Augsburg Fortress in 1999. In journal entries, conversations, prose and prayers they described the first five years of living with Bob's disease.

Now, as the journey continues – a journey of the heart, mind and spirit - Anne has written this collection of poems to explore the feelings of both patient and caregiver. There are poems of loss and grief, certainly, but there are also vital undertones of hope.

The collection is meant to promote understanding and support for the many families and communities that are caring for patients with dementia. Proceeds from the sale of the book will be donated to the Minnesota/Dakota Alzheimer's Association.

GROWING DOWN
Poems for an
Alzheimer's Patient

Anne Simpson

2008
Calyx Press Duluth

ISBN# 0-9772376-9-9

Copyright © 2008 Anne Simpson
Book Design copyright © 2008 Cecilia Lieder

To Bob

Table of Contents

Table of Contents

I. DIAGNOSIS

Photo by Millicent Harvey

SCRAPBOOK

We cut out shining scraps of time
to paste,
like stars,
on black indifferent night.

Our local doctor suspected that Bob had pre-senile
dementia for several years before he was formally diagnosed
with Alzheimer's disease by the Mayo Clinic. He was 62.

At first, the news did not dramatically affect our lives. We
lived in the small community of Grand Marais on the north
shore of Lake Superior where we had many friends, a good
support system and a nurturing physical environment. We
were able to stay involved in community affairs, to visit our
families and spend precious time with grandchildren, even
to take extended vacations.

Bob understood what was happening to him. He talked
about it openly to individuals and to groups. Together we
wrote a book about the first years of our journey, *Through the
Wilderness of Alzheimer's: A Guide in Two Voices,* published by
Augsburg/Fortress.

Though our pace was slow and life became gradually more
and more confining, we learned to pull over sometimes
and fully appreciate the moment. Though there were
definitely times of fear and anger and deep sadness, Bob was
determined to show us that there were also "blessings" in his
disease.

SILVER ANNIVERSARY

On the first walk we took together
you held my hand
and told me about the stars.

You pointed at Orion and the Big Dipper,
identified the planets...
I paid no attention.

I was aware only of your hand,
how rough it was and calloused,
how gently it fit into mine

as it fits me now
when you reach out to lead me back
through all the broken memories
to dreams and stars

till, in the darkness,
I'm surprised
to feel shy again with you.

AT THE BEACH

I often wonder about your mind --
how it feels for you,
what it's like inside your head.

Is it like a seagull soaring away from your body,
darting from one thought to another
swooping to gather someone else's crumbs?

Is it like the rocks
heavy, earth-bound, passive,
warmed by the sun,
collecting nourishment in small pools of water
or patches of moss?

Is it like the waves
lap... lapping the shores of consciousness?

You say the answers come
clear, distinct sometimes
and then, out of nowhere, a fog
blows in and lifts them out of sight.

You say, "All I want to do is
think a little more... but it all goes away.
I'm surprised how fast it goes away."

You say it's like a wave that
rolls in high and full of promise,
then starts to crest out
of rhythm
and spends itself too early.

You can't control the rhythm of your mind now.
You don't know where it will swoop or fly.
You can't sleep away the heavy weight inside your head.

You used to dream that you would
wake up in the morning
and be well.

What do you dream now, I wonder...
Where in the mind fog is your beacon?

You point past the rocks
above the lake
to the clouds,
the high thin ribbons of clouds.
"Look!" you say
"Isn't that the kind of sky where God should be?"

HERE AND NOW

We have a morning
to sit on black ledge rock
splintered from mountains,
smoothed and polished by centuries of
wind and rain and ice.

We have an hour
to look at the lake
where blue dappled waves
break the sun into tiny stars
and sprinkle them at our feet.

All I can know of mountains
is this warm, wet rock.
All I can see of sun
is in this star-drenched moment
here, with you.

PARADOX

The more we lose
the more we appreciate what we have,
the simpler it all becomes.

Like trees after a long winter --
stripped of dreams
passion spent --
we are rooted in rich damp soil,
exposed to warming sun.

It is not the abundant gold of summer
that comforts us now
nor the amber harvest,
but a suspicion of daffodils.

ONE OF THOSE DAYS

On the table
three perfect asters
grace our autumn supper.
I surprised them this afternoon
hiding in the brown grass
of our meadow.

Dusk comes early now
so we light candles,
then heap our plates with harvest:
cabbage, squash, tomatoes,
fresh bread...
I pour wine, cool and dry.

Today I washed windows,
tucked our spent garden under winter cover
and took a long walk with the dog
through woods where orange and yellow leaves,
flickering like flame,
warmed the cool breeze.

This was a day when
all surprises were good
and time flowed so easy
that I would like to clasp and
hold it tight against winter.

But, reluctantly,
I open my hand to
fondle the memories and give them freedom

to waft into corners of my mind
and settle there,
to rise again
in wisps,
like wood smoke,
some dark December night.

AFTERNOON OFF

We used to take time out
to lie in bed
all afternoon.
We would make love,
we'd laugh and talk...

lying on your side,
propped on an elbow,
head cupped in the palm of your hand,
you would look down at me
and gently draw maps with your finger
on my moist warm stomach.

We'd let the phone ring,
the doorbell go unanswered.
We'd whisper and giggle in our privacy,
then get up, smoothe rumpled sheets
and go about our duties of the evening
with light steps.

Now, afternoons in bed
are meant for naps.
We sleep back to back...
but once in a while,
when you turn over and
gently rest your arm upon my waist
I think you must remember.

Even if your breathing is
regular and slow,
even if your eyes are closed,
somewhere deep inside
you must be smiling still

because,
after all these years,
your hand still finds its way
across my stomach.

DAFFODILS

One day in April
the high sun catches us by surprise.
The air is warm,
streams tumble over their banks,
the earth is fragrant with spring.

Before the trees come into bud,
before the crocus pokes its purple head
through the damp soil,
we know...

It's time to pack away our grey and black,
to bring out spring clothes
that splash our days with color.

It happens suddenly
like that day so many years ago
when you bought an armload of daffodils at the store
and presented them to me
with a smile as bright as the sun.

FINDING HOPE

For months
my soul has been in winter,
hardened by ice
deep and cold and strong enough
to support all the worries of the day
standing there at once.

They shuffle through my mind
grumbling, shifting weight,
bundled against hope
like all the bitter women
I resolve not to become.

Now, suddenly,
you smile at me
the way you used to do --
eyes soft and twinkling,
mouth turned up at one corner --
and you reach out your hand.

I hold it till
I feel the sun grow warm,
feel hope bubble to the surface once again
from those dark waters
where poems, sluggish, swim.

THE MAZE

When we were young
we used to argue,
cry or sulk for hours
and then make up with painful joy.

In those tempestuous times
I might have wished for days like these --
quiet, bland
predictable days.

Yet, as I wander through the maze
of household chores
guiding, bathing, dressing, and feeding
I long for you to surprise me,

with a spark of love
or anger
that would flare up
to light my way home.

BOB'S PRAYER

All you ask for is hope --
hope that tomorrow will be
better than today,

hope that your children will grow
to understand,

hope that I will be here
always
to care for you.

Hope that you will belong
and be respected
and be safe
in your home,
in your community.

Hope that you have wisdom to share,
that endurance will knit life together
as your skills unravel.

And if I can give that hope
when I find it hard to give,
then we are doubly graced.

ONE STEP AT A TIME

Each step is a commitment to the future.
One after the other you lift a foot,
pause...
pull back

then lurch forward,
clutching my hand,
dragging me over the invisible threshold
from resignation to hope.

PASSING THE STORE WINDOW

I see that the sweater I've admired for months --
the colorful one that would look good
with skirts or jeans --
has gone on sale.

It would not make me young
or pretty or thin again
or garner an invitation that I could accept.

It would not make your disease go away
and it would cost money better spent on your care
or given to those with no sweater at all.

It will not drive away the chill of losing you
as fall succumbs to winter,
but I think I will go in and try it on,
anyway.

BEACHCOMBER

He trudges through moist, heavy sand
walking the beach,
walking the golden beach.

Azure waves crest above his head
amazing him with their color,
tempting him with their power
to drown uncertainty.

Deliberately,
he sets his shoulder to the wind,
rolls up his trousers
and wipes the dark glasses that soften
late afternoon glare.

The old straw hat scrunched down around his ears,
trash bag tied at his waist,
he begins.

He collects debris
brought in on the high tide
as if he could gather together
all his wasted hours
and discard them,
forgiven,
before the sun goes down.

The old man trudges...
bending and straightening,
sorting and confusing...

determined to save a planet,
to redeem a life,
to sweep this one small stretch of beach
and make a gift of it.

SPRING FOLLY

It is time to throw caution to the winds,
open my fist and scatter promises
of corn, oats, marigolds...

but, winter-blanched and weary,
I clench dreams
as they slip through my fingers.

Out of season,
I want to gather in
all the grain and chaff of you,

to hoard our treasure,
protecting it from thieves and moths,
storing memories in big new barns.

WISHING STONES

The air is soft today,
the sun so warm and breeze so gentle
I lull myself into thinking
it will always be so...

winter just an illusion,
evaporating with summer zephyrs.
Never again will I wear boots or hats or heavy jackets;
never will howling lake winds drive me inland.

I stoop over the cobblestone beach
to search for "wishing stones" --
special red agates with a white ring
all around the middle.

When I find one, I close my eyes and make a wish;
then I throw it far out into the water,
into the lake, sparkling blue and calm,
into water that will never turn to ice.

QUIET IN THE LIBRARY

Here on the shelves
are sentinels of your past,
guarding memories of
all the hours you spent reading
in this room

sprawled in your shapeless chair,
pipe in hand
feet on the worn brown hassock
while sun lit the windows behind you
or light beamed
through dark evenings
from the lamp on your cluttered oak table.

Your books,
gathered in disarray,
were good friends who comforted
and challenged you.

But good friends change
or move away
or die
and connections are broken,
like those that linked your sight
to understanding.

So now the books stand
stiff in colorful formation:
fiction, non-fiction, philosophy...
waiting for you to
put them at ease,
gently to pull one out of order and
wrinkle the starched white pages
with your thumb.

WINTER'S COMING

When the night turns chill, I am dreaming --
deep dreaming
of our old farm,

its green hills and sheep
and children.

You stand beside me
with your hand on my shoulder.
Even in sleep,
I can feel the warmth.

A gentle tug about my feet
rouses me.

You are awake,
staring down the blackness,
feeling a chill that I don't know.

You tuck the extra blanket
round us both
to shield me until dawn.

HUMMINGBIRD

I soar and dip into deep red blossoms,
wings constantly in motion,
beating away fear

so I can take what I need
of the bittersweet nectar --
and only what I can absorb --

to keep me hovering near you
on those days when I want
to swoop and fly away.

UNANSWERED QUESTIONS

You toss in the night,
squeeze your pillow and cry,
"What can I do?
Who am I now?
Where are you?"

When we are children we think adults know all the answers,
when we are adolescents we find them ourselves.
We will never be so wise again.

We may spend our lives tapping the mysteries
of who we are and why we are here
but we will never understand,

so take my hand, come sit by the window --
let's have a cup of tea.
A blazing sunrise paints the snow pink.

TRANSFORMATION

There comes a day in August
when we shrug on a sweater,
when we notice a yellow cast to leaves in the woods
and realize how much the evenings have shortened.

On that day we know:
no matter how warm and bright the days to come,
no matter how blue the sky or how gentle the breeze,
summer is gone for good.

Autumn is a lengthening of the dark --
like progressive disease,
each day better than the next.

But the gold and red
that blaze on the hill
will warm us as we walk by the lake
until the last wet wind blows all the radiance out.

It's then we might notice the sturdy pines
we overlooked before,
scattered on that hill.

Roots wound round and through the rock,
they quietly await their season of beauty,
branches spreading wide
to receive the dazzling shroud.

NEW VISIONS

We hang on to the tag ends of dreams as they
float away from us
into the very atmosphere that gave them birth --
wisps of ideas,
threads of possibility unraveling.

We unfold memories with the morning paper,
stir them into our coffee,
wrap them around our shoulders
to comfort and remind us that

once our step was sure,
our path was clearly marked:
This way to happily ever after.

Nothing is clear now.
We have wandered off the path,
lost our way, seen new visions;
we have confronted fears,
found joy in unexpected byways...

a warm boulder to support our back,
the alchemy of sunlight turning moss to emeralds
and, just when the trail seemed
most dark and narrow,
a clearing round the bend.

We gather our belongings --
our people, our places,
our deepest faith.
We hold them loosely,
palms open, fingers entwined with hope.

BLACK ICE

Relentless winds
sweep light snow
off the streets and sidewalks

so, even when I hold tight
to your arm,
you fall heavily

on the black ice
we didn't see,
couldn't know was there --

the way we slipped
all those years ago
on the diagnosis of dementia.

TEST OF FAITH

I rattle the clouds with words
to shake You loose
only to find,
when I am hoarse at last
that You were always here.

You were in my tears,
in the crying that enters chaos
without trying
to makes sense of it,
swirling me around to
touch the Holy at its core.

Tears are the prayers I cannot pray
deeper than sighs,
too deep for words,
quieter than silence --
a cloudburst of calm.

II. GROWING DOWN

Photo by Millicent Harvey

BOB'S POEM

Of me there is three —
the one I am
the one you see
the one I want to be.

One day, when I took Bob for a check-up, our local doctor
motioned me aside and very gently said, "It's time." I
knew what he meant. It was time for us to leave our small
community and move to Duluth where we would have more
services available for help with Bob's care. It had been our
contingency plan for almost six years.

We went to a continuing care community on the campus
of St. Scholastica. There was adult day care available for
Bob as well as additional help from some wonderful college
students. We participated in monastery and college events,
and we lived within a community of lively senior citizens.

As the disease progressed, inevitably, it took over more
of our lives. Some of the changes and losses were painful
indeed – especially Bob's loss of vision. Bob was aware of
what was happening to him; he said that he was "growing
down." But still we were lucky because for almost four more
years the decline was so gradual that I was able to keep Bob
at home.

BEFORE I WAKE

In early morning
you come to me again —
step firm,
eyes blazing,
smiling as you wrap me in your arms
where I feel safe at last and warm,

until I turn over,
tangled in the sheets,
and struggle not to wake.

In early morning,
the veil is thin between hope and possibility,
between the grey gauze of dreams
and the stark white china cup
I fill with steaming tea.

THE BIRTHDAY BALLOON

Your birthday was two months ago.
The balloon that hugged the ceiling in your den
is losing energy and
showing its age.

It drifts through empty rooms,
rising and falling with daily currents,
so anywhere you go --

when you try to find the bathroom,
or sit at the kitchen table
or settle into your chair to take a nap --

you bump into "Happy 70,"
a gaudy red and gold reminder
that time has gone too quickly.

I try to remember
when we first met
and you could navigate your life without a compass,
when your eyes had light behind them
and your smile was confident.

I try to remember
what you were like
before your mind was pricked by disease,
before life began to leak from your body
and leave you flat.

Then I imagine that your spirit has escaped,
and seeped into the walls,
that it hovers in these rooms
and follows me
though I cannot see it.

Sometimes it surprises me
with a presence on my shoulder
or a gentle nudge
that makes me turn
and catch you
smiling at me,
plump and bright with recognition.

APRIL ON THE LAKEWALK

I'd like to hit the boardwalk at a run,
stride briskly along the lake —
three miles to the harbor and back —
swinging my arms to the sky
and stretching my winter-weary legs.

I'd watch the seagulls circle and swoop,
thank them for coming home,
and, when I was tired, I'd lean back
against the huge warm boulders
and listen to the waves sing plaintive lullabies.

But I feel your hand in mine holding back
as our dog on the leash in my other hand strains forward,
so I mince my way along the boardwalk
slow... slow... quick, quick --
dancing sideways between the seasons.

FULL MOON

A friend calls late at night.
"Have you seen the moon?
Don't miss it."

I rouse you and
bundle us up,
we hurry down three narrow flights of stairs,
out of the apartment building
to where the sky expands.

There she is!

Huge and close and white,
a halo burning all around her
then an aura, shimmering red and green
and another soft white ring
smudging into dark, star-lit sky.

I've never seen a moon like this.
"Isn't it beautiful? Look there."
I point up, turn your head,

you say "and there..." (pointing to the street lamp)
"and there..." (the stop sign in the parking lot)
"and there..." (the radio tower on a distant hill)

You look down and make circles with your finger
 in the air above your feet
"It's everywhere!"

COFFEE BREAK

Across a small round table
in the coffee shop,
the two white heads
bend toward each other.

Slowly sipping from big frothy mugs,
he does a crossword puzzle
while she pages through a book
she might have bought next door.

Comfort drapes around their shoulders
like an old sweater,
warming the space between them
and filling in wrinkles.

We used to sit like that on evenings at home
in silence,
reading or writing or staring into space
without translation.

Sometimes,
when you'd reach absently for your coffee cup
on the table by your chair,
I'd caress your hand

as the old man taps hers now,
lightly,
to tell her that it is time to go.

She smiles with a radiance it pains me to recall
as I brace myself to pull you up
and prod you,
shuffling,
out the door.

THE WOODEN BOX

It's time for you to leave adult day care
but the doorway is blocked by wheelchairs and walkers,
by loved ones helping clients with their hats and coats,
so I call to you
as I weave my way through the crowd,
"I'm here."

You turn toward my voice --
eyes unseeing, face shining.
Slowly, you get up,
stand tall and straight as you are able,
then with regal shuffle, make your way to my side
holding a gift in your outstretched hand.

You carry it as proudly as a little boy
bearing a gift to his mother.
"I made this!" you beam.
"I made it for you."

Wrapped in gaudy red ribbon and a half-tied bow
is a small green wooden box
with a glass heart on top.
You have sanded and painted and polished it,
"with some help," you admit.

With a stab I remember other gifts:
the flowers you carefully picked from the garden,
cards and clever poems and valentines,
the wool sweater you chose for our first winter together,

the wedding ring
I will keep forever
in this little green box
with my name misspelled on the side.

END TIMES

Tomorrow our friends will drive away from this Great Lake,
turn east to the ocean and the land of their belonging.

I want to celebrate this last walk on the beach:
our Border Collie -- head up, tail wagging --
finding a stick and bearing it to us,
dropping it on the foot of anyone
who has not tired of her game.

These two men strolling arm in arm,
communicating in silence
their importance to one another
for almost fifty years.

We women, chattering and laughing
like schoolgirls at some silly reminiscence,
at the sacred absurdity of our connection
through space and time.

But even as I smile at her antics
I can anticipate the absence of our old pet;
as I rejoice in their company,
I mourn the coming separation from our friends.

Yet the one in whose honor we gather
walks with us, not knowing where we are
or why we are here,
and he savors every moment,
forging with his spirit
bonds that have splintered in his mind.

AS YOU WERE

Your family remembers you,
their father and grandpa,
favorite uncle,
their tagalong cousin,
baby brother...
They press their memories
in mental scrapbooks
to cherish and pass on.

Your friends remember, too.
They tell your stories,
laugh at adventures you shared,
patch your ragged present
to their past.

But even when I hear the stories
or study photographs
I cannot find my way back to you.
Try as I might,
I no longer remember
when you could tie your shoes.

MOODS

Yesterday you woke up crying.
You wandered around the bedroom till dawn,
then retreated to your favorite chair and sat.
Sulked.

You wondered who I was,
said you were sorry you married me.

Today you slept till seven.
You followed me around like a puppy,
slopping wet kisses on my face and neck,
coming up behind me and strangling me with hugs.

Dear Stranger,
with moods as unpredictable as winds of the spirit,
where did you come from?
Where did my beloved go?

A FRIEND IN NEED

It is early morning.
Joel calls to say that Deb is sick,
the lunch we planned today
will have to be rescheduled.

I am very disappointed!

Then I picture my dear friend
writhing in wrinkled sheets —
face ashen, hair matted,
bucket within reach —

and here is my compassionate response:

I think, "Oh, God!
It must be wonderful
to have a husband
who can make a phone call!"

LITURGY

Repeated tasks order my day,
nights are silent chaos.

Poems that never see daylight
toss about.
Prayers are
dull arrows shot from a full quiver,
falling short of target,

unless there is a poem
in your freshly ironed shirt;
unless guiding you
to the toilet, the table, the chair, the bed...
feeding, bathing, dressing, and undressing you
can touch the heart of God.

NIGHTMARE

In the middle of the night
you are standing in the bathroom,
pajamas bundled about your knees,
looking around for the toilet
inches behind you
as if it has moved in the hour since you were last here.

You have awakened from sleep
on the bed you cannot name
in the room to which you cannot retrace your steps
because you remember what you need to do.
But when you wash your hands in the sink
you don't know the man looking back from the mirror.

ANTICIPATION

Tippy and I sat together on the hill
outside the office,
waiting for the doctor
to take her in.
The sun was bright.
Her thick black coat was warm where I stroked it
as she rested her heavy head in my lap,
eyes dull, laboring to breathe.

We both knew it was time for her to go.
The vet was gentle,
her death so peaceful and dignified
that I would want my own to be like that,
as I would wish for my beloved
to escape this long, slow wasting of his mind and body,

until I remember the emptiness
that surprised me
when she was no longer there
demanding my attention.

I waited for her to nuzzle my arm and wake me in the morning,
watched for her under my feet all day.
I called for her before I took my walk

and when I was in the kitchen,
over and over I glanced toward that sunny corner
where she was supposed to lie --
ear cocked, one eye open --
hoping for me to drop a crumb.

ROCK GARDEN

Sometimes in the morning
you help me dress you,
suddenly remembering how to wear a shirt.
Or in the evening you recite your bedtime prayers.
These moments of loveliness surprise me
where I least expect them,

like the bluebells that
refuse to grow in my garden,
though I water and fertilize them well,
and instead brave gales from the lake,
taunting me,
poking up from crevices in bare rock.

MAY ON THE LAKEWALK

Young girls wear tank tops and shorts
as they jog or bike or soar solo on their rollerblades.
Old women, bent and bundled, walk stiffly in pairs
stopping to enjoy the view.

I leave my jacket and hat and gloves in the car,
snap a leash on the dog
and stride as briskly as I can
in my sweatshirt --

bright yellow --
because I am tired of grey,
I'm tired of winter,
I'm tired of being old.

Not long ago on such a day
we scrambled to the Lake,
watched in awe as seagulls swooped,
listened to waves quietly lap the shore.

You rested your hand on my knee
or gently wrapped your arm around my shoulder
as I relaxed against you, and we
warmed our backs on black rugged rock.

But that was before your step became unsteady,
before you clutched my hand everywhere we went
and spoke to me in echoes.

It was back when not speaking was comfortable,
back when I didn't walk alone.

RETURN TO GRAND MARAIS

If I had known it would be our last trip,
would it have made any difference?

Would I still have tugged your arm
to hurry you across the street,
down to the beach
so we could watch the fog
playing tag with sun
and hear waves catch the breakwater
beyond the lighthouse?

Would I, instead, have
glanced at people on the sidewalks
searching for familiar faces
in the tourist crowd,
taken time to admire building renovation,
noticed the bright flowers
splashing from pots on every corner?

If I had known that a long trip
would make you so restless
that you'd fidget with your seat belt
and open the car door while we were driving --
known that I could not take you unattended
on another outing --

would we have sat on the warm cobblestones
dangling our feet in the water
till they grew numb?

HERE I STAND

Recently,
when we weren't looking,
a door slammed shut
on the cluttered room behind us.

Strewn across the floor
were all our lasts.
We stepped out of them,
not knowing

there would be no more car trips,
no more walks in the woods,
no concerts or parties or plays.
We wouldn't eat in a restaurant again
or get a full night's sleep...

Now I stand naked
in a stark white room
my firsts hanging neatly at the other end,
a long cold walk away.

THE WELL

The well on the side of the road
beckons tired and dusty pilgrims
and I long to sit on its cool stone ledge,
lower the stained wooden bucket,
slowly raise it
and let us drink our fill,

spilling water over my chin
onto my sticky shirt,
bathing my face,
rinsing my hair.

I long to take off your shoes,
soak your swollen feet
and sit in the shade with you
for all the afternoon.

But I am foolish and so afraid to rest
that I ladle only a cup for the journey,
then lead us,
stumbling and thirsty,
toward the dusk.

THE PUZZLE

I can't remember who I was
before I was tired,
or who you were
when you were whole,

or who we were
before we became
locked pieces of jigsaw
without a frame.

I can't remember when I looked forward to morning,
or when you could undress yourself and come to bed
so we could lie entwined and sleep in peace.

I can't remember peace.

FOR SALLY

Her loved ones
take turns in the hall,
making short visits to the noisy hospital room
where she lies behind a dingy partition --

cold scraps of a meal
on the bedside table,
lukewarm water on the tray,
her fragile life fed through tubes and monitors.

I wanted her to die
surrounded by her family
in a large room
full of sunshine

with lace at the windows
colorful chintz and roses,
thick carpet,
soft music...

But she won't notice any more,
she closes her eyes and purrs like a kitten.
"It's all right," she says.
"I can see in the dark."

III. END STAGE

Photo by Laura Crosby

ALISON'S POEM

Bob

    has alshimers
is gentle and kind
is blind but loving
    loves sweets
        is tall
loves sugar coated pecans
used to be a pastor at
        my church

Alison Leslie, age 10

On the fateful day when finally I had to place Bob in the
dementia unit of our care community, I could not have
guessed that even more painful days were ahead of us.
Bob was seeing hallucinations, he was agitated, scared
and combative. The Alzheimer's diagnosis was tweaked to
include Lewy body disease, explaining the behavior so out of
character for this gentle soul.

He was not allowed to stay in Duluth and so our journey
through the wilderness brought us, in fits and starts, back to
the Twin Cities. Bob is in a special facility in Rogers and I
live in St Paul (an hour away), near the neighborhood where
we began our married life. This arrangement is not nearly as
convenient as what we had in Duluth but it is the best we
can hope for, and Bob is getting wonderful care.

He would rejoice to know that "blessings" of this disease
still are unfolding: we are close to our families and we have

reconnected with friends who have not seen him in years.

Bob is in ministry still, teaching us patience and acceptance. He is dying a gracious death. There were several years of high anxiety and constant chatter but he is more peaceful now. He talks very little but he says "Good, good." He says, "Thank you " and "I love..."

Even as he approaches the end of his long struggle with dementia, he can give love and he can receive it. He is still here!

WINDOWS OF THE SOUL

Before I knew your name, I loved your eyes --
the way they looked right at me when we met,
the way they twinkled as you reached out your hand,
the way the blue darkened when we started talking
and I asked a question that you took seriously.

I remember still the quiver that I felt
as you moved closer,
smiled,

nodded your head and frowned in concentration,
listened.

Now your eyes are closed most of the time,
and I am the one who listens.
As you chatter on and on,
I try to snag a word, a phrase
that I can repeat to bring you back.

Today, settled in your big recliner for a nap,
you open your eyes --
still blue, still clear,
but blank and unfocused, as if
you are asking the questions now.

You are safe, I say.
You are loved.
You don't know who says the words
but they comfort you.
You close your eyes and sleep.

MISTAKEN IDENTITY

You don't know me from the chair
you are stroking,
"Ohhhh....Ummmm..."

The woven mohair blanket
thrown over its back
is soft as my bathrobe

and you don't see
that I am behind you,
standing in the doorway.

When I say, "Time for bed,"
it is a statement --
not an invitation.

You have forgotten the distinction
but not the warmth.
Never the warmth.

HANDS ACROSS TIME

1.

Your hands are fish fins,
rotating fans,
butterflies...
they flit, flop, circle away from your body.

You watch them
detached,
to see
if they can grasp words out of the air,
catch a memory and
fondle it for you,

lift you into the sky
or release you
from this earth
into some deep warm sea
where you are swimming.

2.

In high school you were a boxer,
the best in your district,
with strength and ferocity surprising
in a boy of such gentle nature.

Still your fists are tight and hard
when I dress you;
I duck and parry,
as you thrust them into the sleeves of your shirt.

3.

The first time I held your hand
it was warm and firm and calloused
from a long day of paddling...

we sat by the campfire
as you pointed out the stars
that guided our canoe
across the choppy waters.

You called each of them by name.

4.

In the wheelchair by a sunny window
you are dozing --
your head slumped forward,
lap robe rumpled,
your feet in sheepskin slippers dangling to the floor.

But you smile when you hear my voice,
that mischievous, one side of your mouth turned-up smile.

Eyes closed,
you lift your hand in my direction
cupping it, to fit in mine.
Your firm calloused hand...
soft now, weak and bony.

Life slips between your fingers,
and rests for an instant
in my palm.

VISITATION

In the Alzheimer's home
where the young mother has come to visit,
her baby is crying.
You hold out your arms.

You sit on a cold, metal, fold-up chair
by the nurse's desk,
sit calmly as you hold the flailing bundle --

purple screwed-up face,
fists and feet pummelling the air,
tiny lungs forming screams
that pierce old deafened ears.

Bent over the child, you sit,
gently rocking,
stroking her,
speaking sounds no others understand.

You murmur the language that comes before speech
that she, so recently arrived,
and you, so close to return,
can speak together.

LACK OF IMAGINATION

I can leave any time,
walk out on two strong legs,
climb in my car
and drive wherever I decide to go.

You must stay put.
Tilted in your wheelchair,
you stare out the window of the nursing home.
Can you see the fresh snow?

Do you know that I'm here?
When I get home, I will choose my own menu,
eat dinner when I am hungry,
select a book to read before I go to sleep,

while you wait to be fed, moved, changed, bathed, and
finally put to bed for another long night,
totally dependent on strangers to understand
the needs you can't express.

I cannot imagine life without choices.
I cannot imagine being you --
and, like you, smiling.

THE END OF DAYLIGHT SAVING TIME

Night comes as suddenly as the darkness descended
on your mind.
Driving home from the care center,
I slip into the stream of tail lights moving
relentlessly forward
like the neurons in your brain that flash but do not connect,
that will thin and thin, as the traffic does,
before we reach the end of our journey.

We, who can decide when the sun should rise,
are powerless to turn back the setting
of patients like you
whose loved ones, like me,
will drive away at day's end
and be surprised by some tomorrow's early dawn.

LIVING ALONE

No muddy boots clutter my closet,
no gloves crusted with sawdust and sweat.
My home smells of lavender and cinnamon,
not burley pipe tobacco.

The sprawling recliner is gone from the living room
and the furniture, covered with flowers
in bright colors you don't like,
is just my size.

The bathroom is free when I want to shower,
the calendar is free of any dates but mine.
The checkbook records my expenses
and there is no debate about values,
no argument when choosing a new car
or deciding which family to visit on the holidays.

I can eat what I want
when I want it.
I can turn up the radio
and talk without interruption on the phone.
I can stay up as late as I please
while you,
drugged and scheduled and bolstered,
lie on your narrow cot.

Now I wear socks to bed
to keep my feet warm,
and I stuff a pillow on the side where you should be.
Sometimes I turn toward it in my sleep, forgetting.

DANCING SCHOOL

The boys in stiff collars line up on one side of the room,
the girls in white gloves on the other.
Miss Propriety, in a long black dress, clicks her castanets
and announces, "Boys' choice."

I head for the bathroom
where I spend most Friday nights from 7-9 pm
because I am the tallest girl in seventh grade,
I am plump, I have pimples and braces,
and no boy I like
could possibly want to push me... left, right, left, right...
around the room.

In my senior fitness class
where we are learning the Salsa,
though I am one of the smallest women in the room,
I still feel clumsy and self-conscious,
swinging my arms left
while all the others go right
and I want to bolt for the door when the music stops...

till I wonder
whether any of these women
who exquisitely maneuver the 1-2-3 tap
ever had a partner like mine
who would glide across the floor in muddy boots,
swoop an arm around her waist
and gleefully waltz around the kitchen.

PARTNERS

The dance begins when I put an arm around your waist
to move you
from the wheelchair to the chair
or from the chair to the bed.

You stomp and flail,
you jerk like St. Vitus
or a teen drenched with hormones,
keeping time to demonic rhythms
drummed through your body by fear.

Sometimes you sit one out.
If you are settled in your recliner,
I pull up a chair.
Gingerly, I touch your hand.

Our fingers lace.
Clumsy and tender,
you fling an arm across my shoulder
as we sit cheek to cheek,
slow dancing to faint strains of hope.

SOMEDAY

Someday --
maybe someday soon --
I shall wake with hope,
ready to get up and move on.

But not today.

So don't tell me that
the sun is warm,
the breeze scented with lilac.
Don't recount my blessings
or remind me to be thankful.

Someday --
maybe someday soon --
I will share your laughter,
tell stories and remember my beloved
as he was.

But today
I'll sit with him and hold his hand,
listen to the shallow, ragged breathing,
watch for life to flicker in sightless eyes,
and wait for a flare of recognition.

BLESSED ARE THE CAREGIVERS

Who day and night tell their patients
patiently
what and who and where they are,

who direct those who can't follow directions,
who guide and gently cajole them,
fib therapeutically and laugh spontaneously,

who give up sleep but never hope,
who give love without expecting to receive.
Blessed are they, the merciful...

and blessed are we
who are not so meek or pure in heart.
Blessed are all who mourn.

A CAREGIVER'S THANKSGIVING PRAYER

We step into the creaky boat
and set sail for a moving horizon.
The seas are rough,
the wind is cold,
food scarce,
fellow passengers sick and unruly.

We embark on the journey for which
there is no chart --
only the stars,
only the dream that we can make a difference,
and faith that the God who guided our ancestors
will call forth the pilgrim in us.

COMMUNION IN THE NURSING HOME

Crumpled in your chair,
hands clasped
in prayer, perhaps,
you tilt toward the soothing voice that reads for you
"I will lift up my eyes..."

Your eyes are closed
but as the pastor breaks bread
and holds it up,
you open your mouth to lustily devour
"the body of Christ."

He tilts the cup.
You smile as
"the blood of Christ"
runs down your chin
and stains the front of your shirt.

Here is the broken Body re-membered,
here two or three who love you are gathered together.
"Give us this day..." the pastor prompts,
you nod
"and deliver us..."

Amen.

GRATITUDE

In the dark corner of your quiet room
you are tilted in the recliner
eyes closed, dozing...

hour upon hour, you mumble to yourself
soft nonsense words
punctuated now and then by "thank you" —
a clear, strong "thank you."

Who knows what fragments your memory is piecing
together,
what important work you are doing?

I weep for the loss of your brilliant mind and bright humor.
I grieve for myself,
the size of my loneliness growing as your presence shrinks.

I pray for peace,
whatever that may mean,
for both of us.

I don't know what else to pray.
But you — voice clear and shining in the shadow --
you know.

RESURRECTION

We shed like dry leaves
our beauty,
our health,
our loved ones,
the places we have belonged,
all such stuff as we are made of.

We wriggle our roots
deep into the soil
from which we came,
to which we will return.

Our branches,
gnarled and bare,
stretch out to bless the world
we cannot hold,
reach to the sky
and wait for spring.

SO THIS IS GRACE

Sitting here
by the kitchen window
in the early dawn
of a February morning,
idly stirring my second cup of coffee,

the heat of the sun
surprises me
and, suddenly,
I realize how long
I have been cold.

FINDING SANCTUARY

I'll close the door softly behind me.
Let the pictures hang straight on the walls,
let gentle dust preserve the piles on his desk.
I will visit this room again.

I will enter quietly,
open the shades,
sink deep into his worn leather chair,
rest my head.

Let the tears come.
I will not be afraid or angry here.
I will feel his hand resting in mine,
I will smell his pipe.

CREDITS

Previously published in *Through the Wilderness of Alzheimer's: A Guide in Two Voices* (Augsburg Fortress 1999): At the Beach, Bob's Poem, Here and Now.

In *The Moon Rolls Out of Our Mouths* (Calyx Press Duluth, 2006): The Birthday Balloon, Early Winter, Full Moon, Here I Stand, Rock Garden, So This is Grace, Spring Equinox.

In *The Area Woman* magazine (Duluth MN Oct/Nov 2002) The Wooden Box.

In " I'm Still Here!" collaboration with photographer Laura Crosby: Ali's Poem, Anticipation, At the Beach, Black Ice, Blessed be the Caregivers, Bob's poem, Dancing School, Early Winter, Hands Across Time, One of These Days, Paradox, Resurrection, Rock Garden, Someday, The Birthday Balloon, Transformation, Visitation, Wooden Box.

ACKNOWLEDGEMENTS

I am profoundly grateful to Bob, my life partner and inspiration. I want to imagine that he would be pleased with these poems and that he would feel that I fairly expressed the "blessings" that he was so determined to discover in this journey through the wilderness.

It has been a joy to work with Laura Crosby, professional photographer and my most amazing cousin, on an exhibit and a book about dementia patients called " I'm Still Here!" 20 of the poems in this manuscript are paired with her photographs for that collaboration and she prompted... well, nagged at me... to collect my other poems. Finally, to make peace in the family, I took the challenge and this book is the result.

I do not know if I ever would have dared to consider myself a poet without my writer's group in Duluth — Deb Cooper, Candace Ginsberg, Ann Niedringhaus and Ellie Schoenfeld. The friendship and encouragement and good humor and stark honesty of these women made me want to write at least one poem a month (and drive two hours each way) just so I could come to our meetings at Sara's Table and enjoy their company – not to mention the hugs, the wine and the sweet potato fries.

Jill Breckenridge has been my trusted teacher, guide, mentor and friend for many years. Her affirmation and her editing expertise have supported me through this project at every turn and she has kept me on track. My thanks to Pat Daugherty for her patient proofreading.

In 2005, Cecilia Lieder of Calyx Press Duluth printed an anthology that our group wrote: *The Moon Rolls Out Of Our Mouths*. I have been involved in her two collaborations of poets and printmakers as well. She has been unfailingly helpful and creative and fun to work with so, of course, I wanted her to do this book and I am very pleased that she could. I would also like to thank proofreader Pat Daughtery, and the wonderful people at Christie Printing for their expertise and patience.

Millicent Harvey has been uncommonly generous to share the photographs she took for the *Smith Alumnae Quarterly* (Winter, 2002).

John Henricksson has shared invaluable advice about writing, publishing and marketing.

To all of you, without whom this book could not exist, a heart felt thank you.

INDEX

Photo by Laura Crosby

Anne Simpson is co-author with her husband Robert of *Through the Wilderness of Alzheimer's: A Guide in Two Voices.* (Augsburg/Fortress)

Her poets' group in Duluth published an anthology *The Moon Rolls Out of Our Mouths* (Calyx Press) and she has had poems and essays in various publications including *The Lutheran, The Woman Today, Coping...with Alzheimer's Disease* from the Mayo Clinic and several chapbooks.

Bob, a minister in the United Church of Christ, was diagnosed with dementia at the age of 60. His decline was very gradual and Anne was able to keep him at home for 12 years. For the last 3 years, he has been in a care facility in Rogers MN. Anne lives in St. Paul. They have 6 adult children and a large blended family.